Theory Paper   Grade 1   2014   A
Model Answers

1   (10)

2 *There are many ways of completing this question. The specimen completion below would receive full marks.*   (10)

3   (10)

(a)

(b)   C E G   F A C

4   (10)

5   (10)

6 (10)

(a) 2nd   4th   7th   8th /   3rd   5th   2nd   6th   1st /
                   8ve / 1st   8th / 8ve

(b)

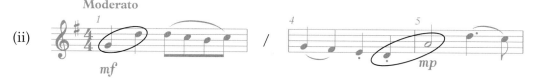

7 (10)

8 (a) (10)
moderate speed / moderately
moderately loud / half loud / medium loud
getting quieter / gradually getting quieter
play the notes detached / jumpy / staccato
go back to the beginning and repeat the section / repeat the passage from the beginning

(b) (10)
   (i)   1

   (ii)

   (iii)   the number of beats in a bar / four beats in a bar
   (iv)   false
   (v)   D

(c) (10)

Theory Paper   Grade 1   2014   B
Model Answers

1   (10)

(a)

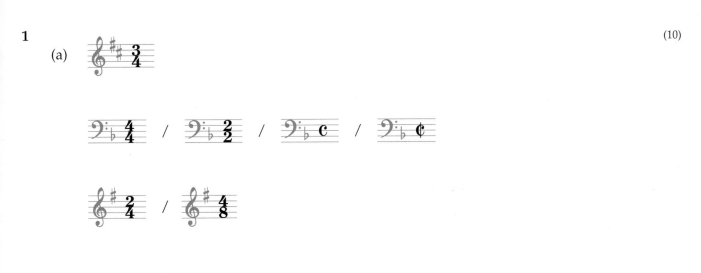

(b)

2   *There are many ways of completing this question. The specimen completion below would receive full marks.*   (10)

3   (10)

4   (10)

Key   D major

Key   C major

Key   G major

5   4th   2nd   8th / 8ve   (10)

5th   6th   3rd

6  (10)

7 (10)

(a)   G E B G D C♯ F♯ A A

(b)   four

8 (a)   fairly quick / quite quick / quick, but not as quick as Allegro   (10)
quiet / soft
getting louder / gradually getting louder
little / a little / a bit / slightly
held back / getting slower / gradually getting slower

(b) (10)

    (i)   3rd
    (ii)   G
    (iii)   crotchet beats / quarter-note beats
    (iv)   minim / half note
    (v)   *legato* (smoothly)

(c)  (10)

Theory Paper   Grade 1   2014   C
Model Answers

1   (10)

(a)

(b)

2   *There are many ways of completing this question. The specimen completion below would receive full marks.*   (10)

3   (10)

4   (10)

(a)

(b)

5 (10)

(a) C E A B♭ C G F D C

(b) two

6 G major   F major   D major (10)
    F major   C major   G major

7 (10)

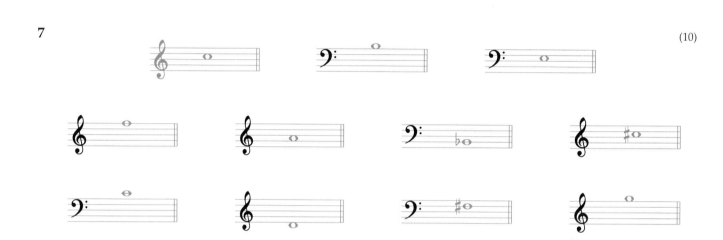

8 (a) at a walking pace / medium speed (10)
    in a singing style
    play the notes smoothly / slur
    very quiet / very soft
    getting slower / gradually getting slower

(b) (10)

    (i) *There are four possible answers to this question. Any of the answers shown would receive full marks.*

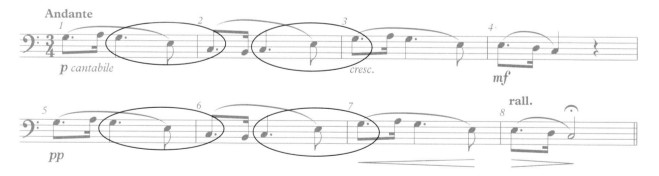

    (ii) 5th
    (iii) minim / half note
    (iv) eight
    (v) 8 / last bar

(c) (10)

Theory Paper Grade 1 2014 S
Model Answers

1   (10)

2   *There are many ways of completing this question. The specimen completion below would receive full marks.*   (10)

3   (10)

4   (10)

G major	D major	C major
F major	G major	D major

5   (10)

(a)   3rd   6th   7th   8th / 8ve / 1st   4th   2nd   3rd   5th   1st / 8th / 8ve

(b)   quaver / eighth note

6   (10)

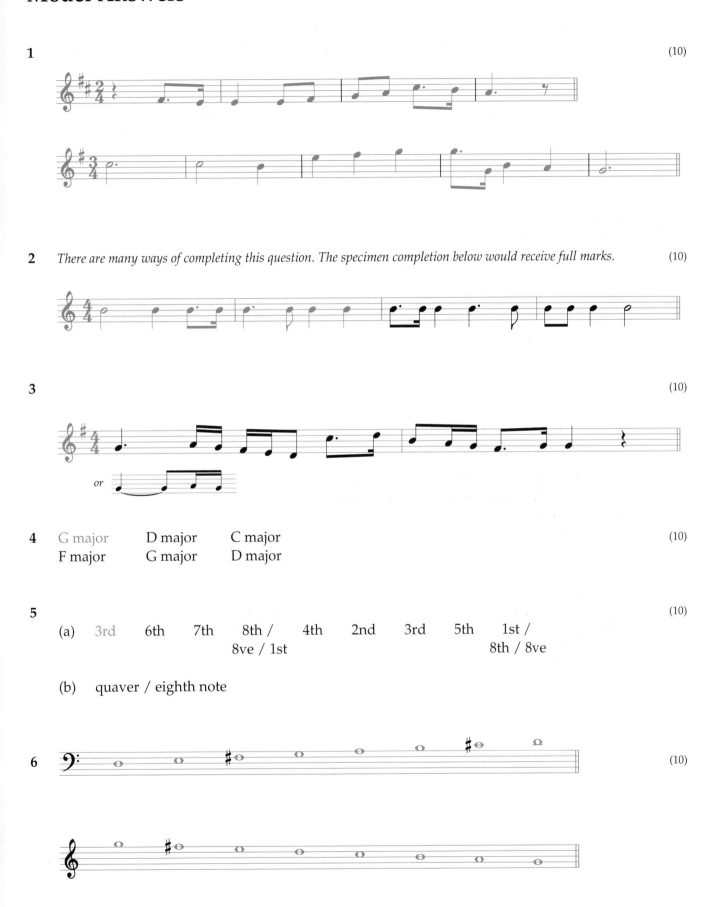

9

7   (10)

(a)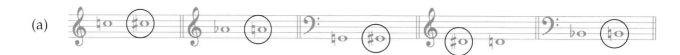

(b)

8   (a)   fast / quick / cheerful / lively   (10)
             the number of beats in a bar / three beats in a bar
             moderately loud / half loud / medium loud
             accent / forced / accented
             getting louder / gradually getting louder

(b)   (10)

     (i)   *The circle is shown in the excerpt reproduced above.*
     (ii)   *The bracket is shown in the excerpt reproduced above.*
     (iii) C / middle C
     (iv)   3rd
     (v)   six

(c)    (10)

Music Theory Past Papers 2014 Model Answers

Model answers for four past papers from ABRSM's 2014 Theory exams for Grade 1

Key features:

- a list of correct answers where appropriate
- a selection of likely options where the answer can be expressed in a variety of ways
- a single exemplar where a composition-style answer is required

Support material for ABRSM Theory exams

ABRSM
24 Portland Place
London W1B 1LU
United Kingdom

www.abrsm.org

ABRSM is the exam board of the Royal Schools of Music. We are
committed to actively supporting high-quality music-making,
learning and development throughout the world, and to producing
the best possible resources for music teachers and students.

ISBN 978-1-84849-712-2